KATE READ
Bright Birds

and their brilliant brains

To all the bright birds I know and love.
With special thanks to Jo and Suzanne for your talent and wisdom.

Consultant: Phil Atkinson, Head of International Research & Principal Ecologist at the British Trust for Ornithology

First published 2025 by Two Hoots, an imprint of Pan Macmillan
The Smithson, 6 Briset Street, London, EC1M 5NR
EU representative: Macmillan Publishers Ireland Limited, 1st Floor, The Liffey Trust Centre,
117–126 Sheriff Street Upper, Dublin 1, D01 YC43
Associated companies throughout the world
www.panmacmillan.com
ISBN 978-1-5290-8818-2
Text and illustrations copyright © Kate Read 2025
Foreword copyright © Megan McCubbin 2025
Moral rights asserted.
All rights reserved. No part of this publication may be reproduced, stored in a retrieval system, or transmitted, in any form or by any means (electronic, mechanical, photocopying, recording or otherwise), without the prior written permission of the publisher.
9 8 7 6 5 4 3 2 1
A CIP catalogue record for this book is available from the British Library.
Printed in China
The illustrations in this book were created using a mixture of collage and monoprint.
www.twohootsbooks.com

KATE READ
Bright Birds
and their brilliant brains

TWO HOOTS

Contents

FOREWORD	8
INTRODUCTION	12
MARVELLOUS MEMORIES	16
CLEVER COMMUNICATION	26
MASTER MIMICS	36
EXPERT ENGINEERS	46
TALENTED TOOL USE	56
INTELLIGENT INVESTIGATORS	70
INDEX	90

Foreword

The world of birds is bursting with vibrant colour, enchanting song and electric energy – some of the best things life can offer. Birds capture the hearts and imaginations of so many people around the globe. They connect us, leading our minds down rabbit holes of wonder, where our curiosity asks simple but fundamental questions like, 'Why do blackbirds sing from the peaks of treetops?' and, 'What does the repetitive call of the cuckoo actually mean?'.

Bright Birds is a beautifully written look at birds from across the world. With every page, you'll be soaking up fascinating details about their biology alongside mind-boggling facts that would surprise even the most experienced of birders. For example, how Fairy-wrens have evolved specialised alarm calls in order to recruit reinforcements from other species during periods of threat. Or how Egyptian Vultures use tools to reach the most inaccessible of meals. The birds are brought to life with stunning illustrations – equally as bold and striking as the species themselves. The pages encourage the reader to appreciate the natural world and invite us to celebrate the beauty, behaviour and cognitive abilities of birds.

I feel the same excitement today watching birdlife as I did as a young child. I have the same feelings of joy and fascination when a Kingfisher darts by (too fast to register in its entirety, but slow enough to leave behind a blurry blue bolt like lightning) or when a Red Kite soars overhead, relying on the rising warm air for lift beneath its angular wings. As much as we now know about birds from modern science and ever-advancing technologies, there remains a magical mystery to them. There is still so much left to uncover, which is one of the reasons this animal group is so interesting – birds keep us guessing, keep us curious, and give us the chance to learn more about ourselves in return.

We are living in a fast-changing world facing a climate and biodiversity crisis. Wild habitats are being restricted and destroyed, our planet's natural systems are shifting, and the seasons are confused to say the least. Birdlife International, one of the world's leading conservation charities, tells us that nearly half the world's bird populations are in decline, with one in eight now threatened with extinction. It sounds scary, and it is. But I am also acutely aware that we have the solutions to help the planet and to save some of its most treasured species. We can all do something to help, starting with appreciating and celebrating the birds that live in our gardens and parks, as well as those further afield around the world.

We only protect what we love – so let's get on with loving the exquisite beauty birds bring to the world; their remarkable intelligence and their captivating songs. It is a wonderful world to be part of, if only we stop, look, and really listen to the life around us.

Megan McCubbin

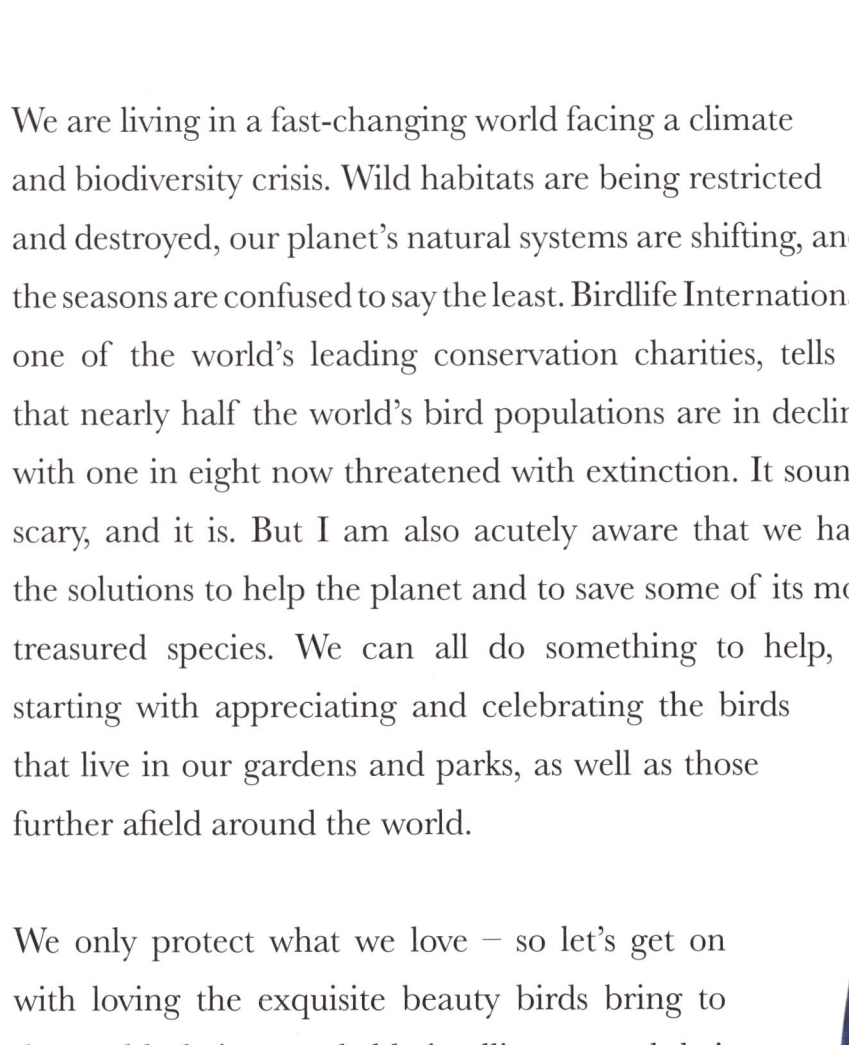

Introduction

Birds can be found almost everywhere on Earth. There are thousands of different species, which come in all sizes and colours, from the teeny-tiny Bee Hummingbird that would fit in the palm of your hand, to the enormous Ostrich that would bump its head on the ceiling if it were standing in your home.

Birds originally evolved from dinosaurs and have been in existence for around 150 million years. They continue to evolve in different ways, adapting and learning new skills to suit new environments. They are able to do this by using their brilliant brains.

All brains are incredible. No matter how big or small, they are vital to make living beings function and are the most complex part of the body. But if someone were to call you 'birdbrain', it would not be meant as a compliment. They would be calling you foolish, suggesting that you have a tiny brain that isn't as clever as most human brains. But perhaps this insult isn't really fair to birds?

Humans have very big brains. The outer layer of the human brain is called the cerebral cortex and is full of deep folds, which maximises the surface area that can fit inside our heads. The cerebral cortex plays a key role in our higher-level functions, such as memory, thinking, reasoning, learning and problem-solving, as well as our emotions and making sense of what we can see, hear, touch, taste and smell. In other words, many of the things that we believe mark us out as special compared to the rest of the animal kingdom, including birds.

However, birds are very different to humans, so their brains have evolved for their needs. We are understanding more

and more about how bird brains work, and seeing how they, too, have good memories, and can learn and problem-solve in different ways.

When it comes to brainpower, what really matters is the number of neurons a brain contains. Neurons are messengers which fire off electrical pulses, telling the body what to do and when. Humans have a huge number of neurons in their brains – 86 billion, which is about the same number as there are stars in the Milky Way.

Bird brains also have a lot of neurons – millions, and in some cases billions, of neurons which work fast and 'talk' to each other constantly. Some of the cleverest species of bird, such as crows and ravens, are at least as intelligent as apes, which have the same-sized brains, but only half as many neurons.

Amazingly, birds can keep their brains alert by making completely fresh neurons whenever they need them throughout their lives. Humans can't do this. We have to make do with exercising the same tired neurons we were born with, so our brains steadily become slower as we get older.

A bird brain is also much smaller and smoother than the human brain. But birds have big brains compared to their body size . . . and they put them to excellent use, often in quite complex ways.

On average, the brains of songbirds and parrots are much bigger relative to their bodies, which means they have room for many more neurons. In some cases, it has been calculated to be about twice as many as other birds, or even as other mammals.

Research into birds and their brains is revealing new information all the time, but it is already clear that a bird brain is a highly developed organ, offering its feathered owner an intelligence and ability to develop skills surprising in a creature so small. Some species, such as corvids and parrots, are especially clever, but all birds have developed their own talents. Birds can be mischievous, playful, inquisitive and problem-solving, just like you. They can communicate, work as a team, even make tools. And they can find their way across longer distances and more accurately than almost any human, without the aid of a map – or a satnav.

Because we see birds all the time, we may not notice just how clever they are, but if you take the time to watch very carefully, you can notice exceptional behaviour in the birds living just outside your window.

In this book I have gathered together some of the brightest birds, and in the pages that follow you will learn about just some of the many, and often unexpected, ways these beautiful miracles of nature use their clever brains.

You will never look at birds in the same way again.

Marvellous Memories

Having a good memory can be a matter of life or death in a bird's world. Relative to their size, many birds have a large hippocampus, the area of the brain which remembers things. These birds have unusually strong memories, which they put to good use, for example to help them defend their chicks, or for finding ways to collect or store food.

Memory is also vital for birds that migrate, helping them to navigate often extraordinary distances across the globe as they travel from their breeding grounds in search of food and warmth for the winter. Birds use various different methods of navigation, but their marvellous memories are key to finding their way between their summer and winter homes with absolute precision. They succeed in arriving at the exact same location every year, which is amazing when you think how far these small creatures have travelled.

Homing Pigeon

Rufous Hummingbird

Clark's Nutcracker

Homing Pigeon
Worldwide

Barn Swallow
Worldwide

Arctic Tern
Antarctic, Arctic, Europe, South America, Australasia

Rufous Hummingbird
Canada, Mexico, USA

Australian Magpie
Australasia, New Guinea

Clark's Nutcracker
North America

Eurasian Jay
Central and East Asia, Europe

Homing Pigeon

The humble pigeon has a brain the size of a peanut, but they are much smarter than you might think. They are superb navigators who can find their way home from hundreds of kilometres away and from any location.

This extraordinary ability has made pigeons very useful to humans over the years. Homing Pigeons have carried messages since ancient times. In New Zealand in 1985, pigeon post became the first regular airmail service between Great Barrier Island and Auckland. A few years later, during the First World War, pigeons were sent across enemy lines with coded messages rolled up in a cannister attached to their ankle. By 1918, the British Army had 20,000 such pigeons; some even received awards for bravery.

Exactly how pigeons achieve these feats is a matter of debate. Some scientists think that they use a spot of a mineral called magnetite in their beak which allows them to use the Earth's magnetic pull; others that neurons in their brain can detect changes in the Earth's magnetic fields to create a sort of map in their mind.

Maybe they hear deep vibrations through the Earth's atmosphere. Pigeons can become confused and lose their way in the path of a jet plane, perhaps because the plane's sonic boom interferes with their hearing.

Or maybe they use their sense of smell to locate their way home. One test suggested that pigeons create a scent map in their brain to guide their way.

One thing is for certain, Homing Pigeons have excellent eyesight and a strong memory. As they fly closer to their home they are able to recognise individual landmarks, knowing where to land with pinpoint accuracy.

Barn Swallow

Barn Swallows make their cup-shaped nests out of mud, straw and their own spit. It takes each pair of swallows a very long time to build their nest, making over 1,000 trips to gather hay, animal hair and mud to construct a solid home. Most birds only use a nest once, but the swallow's nest takes so long to construct that they reuse it the following year. A really successful swallow's nest will be used for a lifetime, which is up to fifteen years.

Swallows don't just have exceptional memories, they can also fly up to 50 kilometres an hour (as fast as a car) and can cover 300 kilometres in a day. They are migratory birds and each season leave their nests in the northern hemisphere to fly south, where they spend half the year. When it is time to return, they don't use a map, instead they have to remember a route, and the exact location of their tiny nest, which could be nearly 10,000 kilometres away. After such a long journey, they are exhausted when they arrive, so instead of wasting energy building a new nest, it makes sense to remember and use their home from the year before.

Arctic Tern

Arctic Terns can fly in their sleep. They are able to rest one half of their brain at a time, keeping the other half working so that they don't crash. This means they can fly for longer.

These endurance athletes of the air have an incredibly long migration and see more summer sunshine than any other bird. They fly from the Arctic to the Antarctic and back again every year, stopping to feed and rest along the way. One has been recorded flying a route of 96,000 kilometres – the equivalent of travelling two and a quarter times around the planet. By feeding as they fly, Arctic Terns are able to fly up to 8,000 kilometres in one go.

Arctic Terns nest in huge groups, or colonies. Young birds learn the coastal route from their parents and the entire colony returns to the exact same nesting ground at the same time each year. Even though individual birds may have wandered thousands of kilometres off their route to find food during the journey, they manage to arrive at the same time as the others.

Rufous Hummingbird

Don't underestimate this miniature bird. It may be smaller than some insects and its brain may be the size of a grain of rice, but it has an exceptional memory.

Hummingbirds beat their wings roughly sixty times per second – so fast it creates their humming sound. That takes a lot of energy and they need to refuel regularly. They also have particularly good colour vision, as well as being able to see ultraviolet light and even different patterns. This helps them spot flowers at a distance so they can regularly fill up on the rich, sugary nectar. Being then able to recall the location of those flowers with the most nectar, and when each flower has been emptied, is essential for their survival.

Rufous Hummingbirds have the longest migration of all hummingbirds. Each year, they find their way from Alaska to Mexico – a journey of over 6,000 kilometres. They are able to remember the exact feeding spots they visited the previous year. If people move the nectar feeders which are sometimes put out for them, the birds will remember and go looking for them. An extraordinary memory indeed.

Australian Magpie

During what is known as 'swooping season', Australian Magpies (a different species to the Eurasian Magpie) become dangerous defenders of their chicks and fiercely attack other birds, animals – and people.

They have very long memories and can remember up to a hundred different people individually. If they have swooped you before, they are likely to attack again . . . even up to five years later.

Australian Magpies live in large groups and will return to the same spot every year, so people who live near nesting birds are advised for their own safety to avoid going anywhere near them during swooping season.

Clark's Nutcracker

Clark's Nutcrackers are super hide-and-seekers. They will each hide as many as 100,000 nuts and seeds in the summer months. When the weather turns cold, they can remember up to 5,000 separate hiding locations (caches), even months after they have stashed their food. Even though the food stores and landmarks are covered in snow, Clark's Nutcrackers can rely on their excellent spatial memory to find their food again.

During the foraging and hiding season, and then again during the winter, this clever bird's brain actually grows temporarily bigger. The part of the brain which is involved in memory creates more neurons to help it recall the hiding places later in the year. This clever form of food storage means that they can plan ahead.

Unlike other birds, Clark's Nutcrackers can hatch their eggs and raise their chicks during winter months because they can feed their young on stored nuts and seeds. The males warm the eggs while the females recover the food from the caches. Not all their food will have survived the winter, so they will check each nut carefully in their beaks and only eat the ones which are fresh.

Birds that cache their food are also vital to keep forests thriving. They can't recover every single hidden nut and seed, so some are left to grow into plants and trees, creating more food for years to come.

Eurasian Jay

Eurasian Jays also have excellent memories. They can hide up to 11,000 nuts in a season and can still remember where they put them up to ten months later. These very intelligent birds often live in pairs. Understanding the benefits of sharing, jays will always share food with their partners, who return the favour.

These clever birds are also able to show incredible patience and self-control. In studies, they have been shown to turn down an immediate food reward and wait for a more nutritious treat instead, if they know that is a possibility. This delayed gratification is a sign of real intelligence and something humans don't learn to practise until they are five years old.

Clever Communication

Birds need to communicate with each other, just as we do. They speak to each other by singing, chattering and making alarm calls, and also by using body language. Some drum their beaks on tree trunks, and others are even known to fashion basic drumsticks to tap out a rhythm. These are all methods that birds use to defend their nests, attract mates and even to find food. So when you are enjoying the glorious sound of birdsong, remember that for the bird, their music is full of meaning.

Western Scrub Jay
Mexico, USA

Great Spotted Woodpecker
Eurasia

Black Palm Cockatoo
Australasia

Greater Honeyguide
Africa

Green-rumped Parrotlet
South America, Caribbean

Blue tit
Eurasia

Rhode Island Red Chicken
Worldwide

Superb Fairy-wren
Australia

Western Scrub Jay

Western Scrub Jays live in pairs and are rarely seen in large groups. They regularly steal from other jays' food stores and are always on the lookout for thieves. If they think their cache has been spotted by a rival, they carefully re-hide their food in a new location.

Despite their usual antisocial behaviour, if one finds another which has died, they raise a huge racket until more Scrub Jays gather. Over and over, they squawk and shriek, flying higher into the branches to encourage more jays to come closer. This behaviour, possibly warning other birds of potential danger, has been described as being like a very noisy funeral. Afterwards, jays that have been gathering food nearby stay away for a couple of days to be on the safe side.

Great Spotted Woodpecker

Woodpeckers drum their beaks on tree trunks to find juicy grubs to eat and to make their nesting holes. But they also use the drumroll sound to communicate with each other. Each species of woodpecker has a different rhythm, as does each individual, which means all the woodpeckers in the forest know who is drumming.

Black Palm Cockatoo

These parrot performers love to play a heavy beat. A rare example of a bird using tools, Black Palm Cockatoos use their strong beaks and claws to craft drumsticks out of branches and seed pods, which they bang rhythmically against hollow tree trunks. Almost certainly designed to attract a mate, individual birds have distinctive drumming styles.

Greater Honeyguide

Most birds are naturally wary of people, but not the bold Greater Honeyguide.

They mainly eat beeswax and are one of very few birds who can digest it, but they need the help of humans to smoke out the bees so that they don't get stung in the process.

In Mozambique, wild beehives are often found high up within the hollows of baobab trees. Local people send honey hunters to gather the rich nutritious honey which is a vital part of their diet. The area they have to search is so huge that it pays to get some local knowledge. This comes in the form of the incredibly clever communicator, the Greater Honeyguide. The local people have developed a mutually rewarding relationship with this bird and their chances of finding a hive are greatly increased by working together.

The honey hunters make a 'brr-hm' call to let the bird know they are ready to follow, and the Honeyguide responds with its own call, flying from branch to branch, leading the hunters to the hives. The hunters then subdue the bees with smoke before cracking open the hives, revealing bee larvae, wax and honey. They take the honey, leaving the wax for the birds. This mutually beneficial relationship goes back hundreds of years, maybe even to prehistoric man, and in different parts of Africa, honey gatherers use different calls to communicate with their local birds.

Green-rumped Parrotlet

These little birds each have their own unique contact call, which acts like a name and is learned from their parents. These names allow parrotlets to recognise their mate, as well as to identify their chicks, which is important because young parrotlets need to be fed by their parents for a further three weeks after they have left the nest.

Blue Tit

In the UK, milk used to be delivered to your door in glass bottles topped with foil lids. In the 1920s, one or two clever Blue Tits and Robins pecked through the foil to reach the cream which rose to the top of the milk. The Blue Tits spread the news to other Blue Tits, and by the 1950s, all over the country they knew the secret. But Robins didn't share their knowledge; instead these territorial birds just chased each other away . . . leaving the Blue Tit population to get all the cream.

Rhode Island Red Chicken

Cockerels (male chickens) make different alarm calls depending on which predators they spot. If they spy a fox, they will stand up as tall as they can, hoping to make the fox think twice before attacking, while calling loudly to warn the rest of the flock. If they see a buzzard or a hawk in the sky, they will crouch down low to the ground as they call, to avoid being captured. They are so clever, they only call to raise the alarm if they are with another chicken. When they are alone, they make the movements but stay quiet so they don't draw extra attention to themselves.

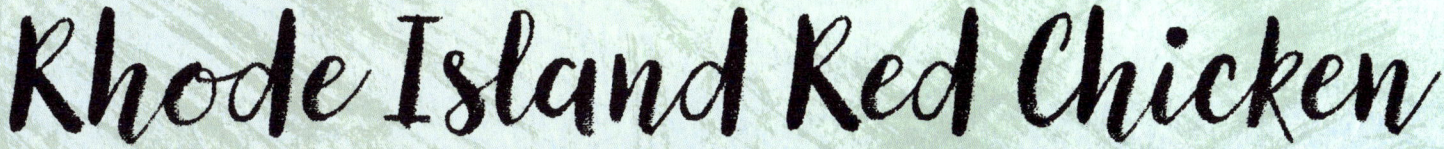

Superb Fairy-wren

There are several species of these brightly coloured little balls of fluff, each living in their own separate communities. Superb Fairy-wrens are locked in a fierce battle with their enemy, the Horsfield's Bronze Cuckoo. These cuckoos lay their eggs in Fairy-wren nests – eggs which look very similar to the those of the wren. They then leave their offspring to be raised by the smaller birds. But warming and feeding chicks takes time and energy which the wrens should be spending to raise their own family, so they are fighting back in surprising ways.

Fairy-wrens aren't born knowing that a cuckoo is dangerous to them. They have to watch the aggressive behaviour of adult birds before they learn what to do, but they learn fast.

Their first line of defence is to mob the cuckoos before they can lay any eggs. Fairy-wrens know they will have more success with the help of other birds, so they have developed a universal language – an alarm call to summon other bird species to join the cuckoo attack. The other birds join in willingly, because the cuckoo is a threat to them, too.

If a cuckoo outwits the mob and does lay an egg in a Superb Fairy-wren's nest, the battle may not be over. All cheeping chicks look very similar in the dark of a domed nest, so the mother Fairy-wren teaches their own offspring a special 'password' call while they are still in their eggs. Each wren family has its own password, which, when the chicks hatch, they add into their begging call. The cuckoo's egg is not laid in time for that chick to learn this secret code, so it cannot make the right sound, and the adult wrens will not feed it. Sadly for the cuckoo chick, this means its own mother's cunning plan was all in vain.

Master Mimics

Many birds are excellent mimics, learning to copy the calls of other birds, but also human and even mechanical sounds. Some can do this with complete accuracy.

Birds which mimic other species do so for lots of different reasons. Sometimes it is to call for help from another species if a predator is near; sometimes to make the predator think there are more birds nearby and thereby frighten them away. They also use their clever copycat abilities in cunning ways to steal food, and even as part of the way they lay their eggs. But the most common reasons are to defend their territory and to find a mate – the birds with the widest repertoire are likely to be the most attractive to prospective partners.

Common Cuckoo
Africa, Asia, Europe

Fork-tailed Drongo
Africa

Superb Lyrebird
Australia

Northern Mockingbird
North America, Mexico, Carribbean

Common Hill Mynah
South Asia, South East Asia

Crested Lark
Eurasia, North Africa

Common Starling
Worldwide

Macaws
South America

Common Cuckoo

There are many different species of cuckoo, and they are all masters of disguise. They lay their eggs in other birds' nests for them to be hatched and raised by others. They have evolved to mimic the size, colour and pattern of their host's eggs so accurately that the host cannot tell the difference.

Cuckoos even mimic other birds' feather patterns. The stripes on their chests are adapted to match the local bird of prey species, such as the sparrowhawk. This disguise helps to scare the hosts from their nest while the cuckoo lays its imposter egg. But it doesn't always work. Reed Warblers have matched the cuckoo's cleverness by learning the difference between the two birds and will mob a cuckoo, but flee from a sparrowhawk.

Female cuckoos will lay up to twenty-five eggs each summer, all in different nests. Timing is everything, and it takes hard work and patience to find the perfect hosts. When they spot a clutch of eggs in an unguarded nest, the cuckoo swoops down and lays an identical egg in as little as six seconds. Then they quickly remove one of the original eggs to avoid suspicion – the owner of the nest will destroy an egg if they realise it is not their own. As they fly away, some cuckoos call out as if laughing – a chuckle that mimics a sparrowhawk's call. This is intended to further distract the host from noticing the new egg.

The cuckoo egg hatches first. Although still blind and featherless, their will to survive is so great that new cuckoo chicks are able to manoeuvre the unhatched eggs, and even any other baby chicks, out of the nest with their wings and legs, leaving themselves as the only mouth to feed.

Eventually, the cuckoo chick outgrows the nest and is even bigger than its unsuspecting and exhausted host parents, who nevertheless continue to feed it. Then, when the time is right, the young cuckoo disappears, flying alone for thousands of kilometres to the warmer climes of sub-Saharan Africa.

Fork-tailed Drongo

The Fork-tailed Drongo is a master trickster. It can mimic the calls of around fifty other birds and mammals, and regularly uses this talent to steal food. Using its keen observation skills, it gains the trust of animals such as meerkats by pretending to keep guard for hawks. It then mimics the cry of a bird of prey and steals the meerkats' food when they run for cover. The drongo is clever enough to know this trick won't work twice, so next time it mimics the meerkats' own alarm call, and makes them run for cover all over again.

Superb Lyrebird

The Superb Lyrebird is an extraordinary performer who can mimic over one hundred different sounds, including children playing, chainsaws buzzing, a radio tuning, car alarms sounding and dogs barking. It clears a space in the forest for a stage and performs the widest range of sounds it can. The bird with the widest repertoire will be the most attractive to female birds.

Younger birds learn the sounds from their elders, as well as by listening to what they hear around them. Their mimicry is so accurate that other birds cannot tell it is a lyrebird singing and not a bird of their own species.

Northern Mockingbird

Northern Mockingbirds can mimic around 200 calls and songs of other birds. They also imitate other animals, such as frogs and squirrels, and sounds such as dripping water and car alarms. The more varied the sounds they can make, the more attractive they are to potential mates.

Common Hill Mynah

The Common Hill Mynah is an excellent mimic of human speech when kept in captivity, but in the wild it makes loud shrieks and gurgles which sound like children playing. These clever birds must learn by listening to their elders, and each region's bird has a different dialect.

Crested Lark

In Germany, one Crested Lark learned to copy a shepherd's command whistles. It then taught all its friends, and the sheepdogs started following the birds' directions instead of the shepherd's commands.

Common Starling

Starlings are noisy and characterful birds who can mimic human speech as well as the calls of about twenty different birds, including buzzards, blackbirds, gulls and sparrows.

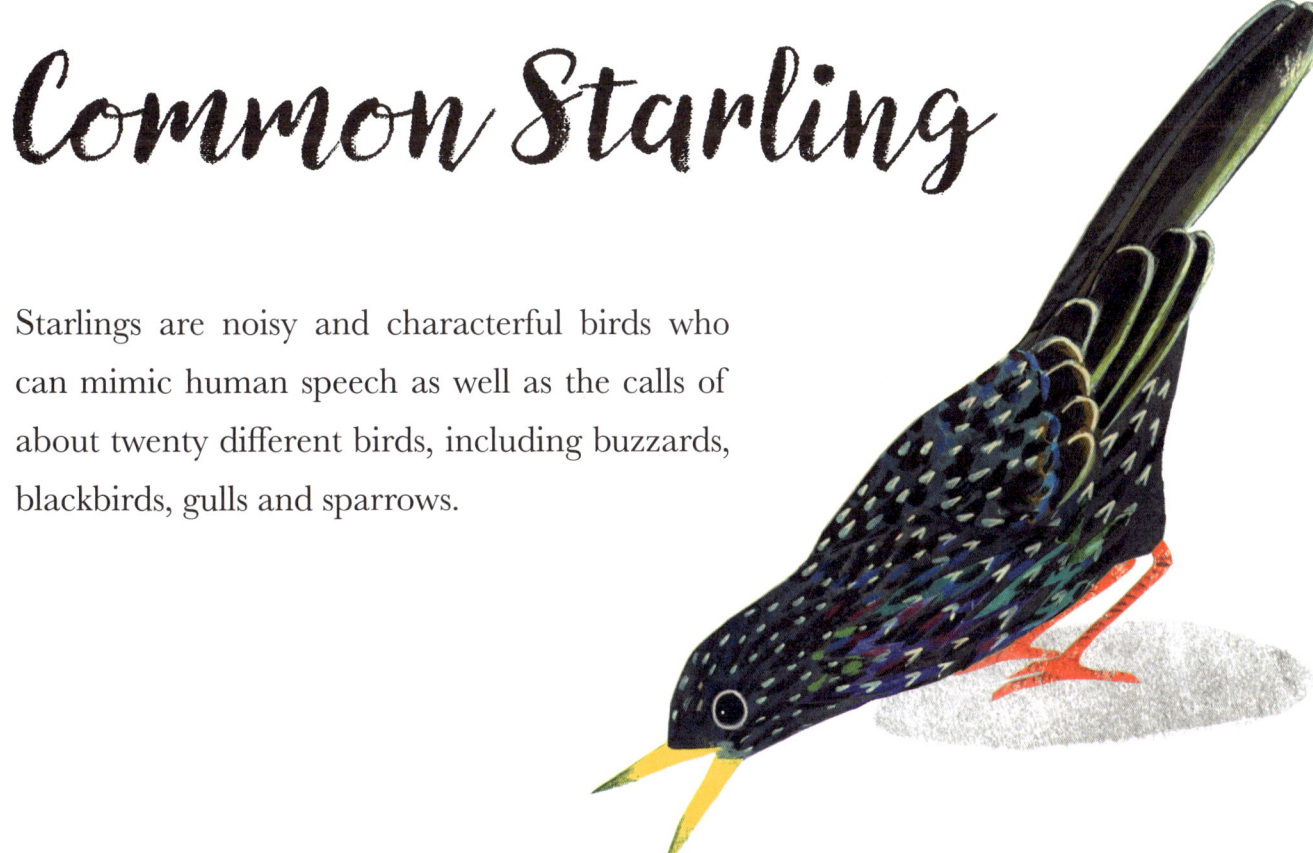

Macaws

Macaws are said to be as clever as a five-year-old child and can live to the ripe old age of eighty. They can mimic human speech easily, using their tongues to form words. All parrots are vocal learners: they listen, remember and repeat back what they have learned almost immediately. They can recall around fifty words and a pet macaw, if carefully taught by a human, understands what they are saying. For example, they are able to ask for particular foods.

Expert Engineers

Crafting a nest takes brainpower, practice and the ability to learn from mistakes. Each nest must suit its environment, providing a warm place for chicks to grow up. It must be safely hidden from predators, whether that be high in the treetops or down in an underground burrow. And, of course, it must be built using easily-sourced local materials, from mud and straw to grass and leaves. Some include sheep's wool, feathers, or even strips of plastic and other man-made materials foraged from humans. In the UK, one swan used a hosepipe lying in someone's front garden as the basis for its nest.

Not all birds build nests in which to lay eggs or to shelter. Male bowerbirds, for example, create surprising structures simply to attract a mate. But they all display a level of engineering skill and adaptability of which any human would be proud.

MacGregor's Bowerbird
New Guinea

Vogelkop Bowerbird
Papua New Guinea, Indonesia

Satin Bowerbird
Australia

Vitelline Masked Weaver
Africa

Common Tailorbird
Asia

Sociable weaver
Southern Africa

MacGregor's Bowerbird

Bowerbirds are the architects of the bird world. They all build differently shaped bowers, which can take up to two months to perfect. The birds who build the most elaborate constructions are the birds with the biggest brains. Their bowers are not built to hold eggs but only to attract female bowerbirds, who make a separate nest elsewhere.

The MacGregor's Bowerbird constructs a tall tower of a bower about the height of a six-year-old child. They decorate it with berries and leaves which they hang all over it. This bowerbird is also a very good mimic and can copy sounds as varied as human speech, wild pigs and running water as part of its display. All in all, they work very hard to prove themselves worthy of a female bowerbird's attention.

Vogelkop Bowerbird

The Vogelkop Bowerbird is a den builder, whose bowers look like huts with pointy roofs such that a fairy might make. It even creates a beautiful front garden decorated with lots of differently coloured piles of 'treasure' consisting of plastic, berries, shells, leaves and flowers, all carefully sorted into colours.

Satin Bowerbird

The adult male Satin Bowerbird has dark glossy feathers and bright violet eyes. He builds an avenue-style bower and takes his time collecting lots of blue flowers, berries and pieces of plastic to display around it. Females and younger males both have olive green plumage and look very similar to each other. The cheeky young males take the opportunity to watch and learn how to arrange the precious blue treasure, but also to trick the older bird into thinking they are female and so trying to impress them. While he is distracted in his performance, the youngsters swoop down and steal his collection from right under his beak.

Vitelline Masked Weaver

Weaverbirds construct extraordinary-looking nests which hang from spiky trees like festive baubles. The nest is started with a knot of grass on a branch, followed by a hanging ring shape. Strips of grass complete the bulbous nest. It takes hours of practice to become a really skilful weaver, and young birds must learn the technique from their elders. The nest uses 1,000 strips of grass and each hard-working bird will build up to twenty nests in a season.

Common Tailorbird

Common Tailorbirds sew their nests out of spiderweb silk and leaves. These tiny tailors use their beaks and feet to wrap themselves in the perfect leaf to check it is supple and big enough, just like a fashion designer would check their fabric. If it is not big enough, they will use one or two more leaves. Then they pierce holes with their super-sharp beaks, before gathering spiderweb silk and plant fibres to stitch together their pocket-shaped nest. Finally, they fill it with a soft lining of feathers or fur. Perfectly camouflaged in a leafy bush, a nest might be held together with around 170 tiny stitches. The female tailorbird is the one who creates the nest, but the male bird will help by bringing her material with which to sew.

Sociable Weaver

Sociable Weavers construct enormous nests. They work as a large flock, constantly maintaining a sort of giant bird hotel. Often these huge haystack-like nests are built on telegraph poles or in trees with smooth trunks to make it difficult for snakes to get in. Some of them are up to a hundred years old.

From underneath, the nests look like beehives, with a lot of entrance holes. Inside, they are cleverly constructed to both keep cool in the hot sun and warm during the freezing desert night. The long tunnel entrances have spiky sticks woven into them to deter predators and there are even some fake entrances to cause confusion.

These incredible structures can hold around 400 birds at any one time, and not only Sociable Weavers. Larger birds, such as vultures and eagles, will live on the top of the nests, and other species, such as Rosy-faced Lovebirds and Pygmy Falcons, will snuggle up in any empty cavities which are warm, dry and protected. These guests are not always welcome, but they can protect their hosts by warning of potential threats such as snakes or honey badgers. This is true community living.

Talented Tool Use

Using tools was once thought to be done only by mammals, but a surprising number of birds regularly use found tools. Some can even use their beaks and claws to construct their own, which they then use in inventive ways to find food.

This behaviour can be seen in the wild, but it has also been demonstrated by scientists working with birds in (often temporary) captivity. This is particularly the case with corvids – the family of birds to which crows, magpies, ravens and jays, among others, belong and the genus often considered to contain the most intelligent of bird species.

Eurasian Nuthatch
Europe

Woodpecker Finch
Galápagos Islands

Blue Jay
Canada, USA, Mexico

Black Kite
Worldwide

Burrowing Owl
North and South America

Black Heron
Sub-Saharan Africa, Madagascar

Green Heron
North and Central America

Egyptian Vulture
Europe, Africa, Asia

Tanimbar Corella
Indonesia, Puerto Rico, Singapore

New Caledonian Crow
New Caledonia

Carrion Crow
Europe, Asia

Eurasian Nuthatch

Nuthatches are busy little birds which can be found hopping up and down tree trunks. They have learned to use a flake of bark as a tool to reach the juicy grubs underneath. Sometimes they even take the best bits of bark with them to use on other trees.

Woodpecker Finch

Woodpecker Finches use twigs and cactus spikes to pick insects out of tricky-to-reach spots. They carefully choose and shape the tool to fit the hole. They are born with this ability, but are clever enough to improve their skills with practice and by observing how other finches use their tools.

Blue Jay

Anting is an unusual bird beauty treatment that many birds, including the Blue Jay, take part in. They sit on the ground in the middle of an ants' nest with wings outstretched and let the ants run all over their body. The ants produce a substance called formic acid in their sting which kills off the parasites that live in the bird's feathers. Birds sometimes pick up an individual ant in their beaks and squirt them like a tube of toothpaste in order to reach all their feathers.

Black Kite

Bush fires are very common in the arid grasslands of the Australian outback. Black Kites, Brown Falcons and Whistling Kites have all been spotted using wildfires to flush out food for themselves. As the blaze spreads, these 'firehawks' fly to the front of the flames and pick off small animals, lizards and insects who are trying to escape. Some birds have been observed going one step further, by dropping burning embers in another area to direct the escaping animals and to keep the flames burning. To have worked out how to do this suggests a very clever brain indeed.

Burrowing Owl

Unlike other owls, Burrowing Owls live underground, in burrows they have dug themselves, or taken over from badgers, prairie dogs or tortoises. Even though they can fly, they prefer to stay on the ground and hop to get around.

Burrowing Owls love to eat dung beetles and other insects. They cover the ground in front of their nests in animal dung that they have collected and wait for their food to come to them.

They also eat small mammals, hoarding hundreds of them in underground larders.

To protect their nests and food supply, they scare away predators by pretending to be a rattlesnake, hissing and rattling while safely hidden inside their home.

Black Heron

The Black Heron spreads its wings out like an umbrella to create its own shade in the hot sun. It can see the fish more easily without any reflection on the surface of the water. Its slow, careful movement and this use of its wings also tricks the fish by encouraging them to hide in the shadow thinking they are safe. This is a great example of a bird using its own body as a tool.

Green Heron

Green Herons are masters of self-control. If they find a bit of bread, instead of eating it themselves, they have learned to use it as bait to attract a fish and catch themselves a far tastier and more nutritious meal.

Egyptian Vulture

Egyptian Vultures use smooth pebbles to crack open large ostrich or bustard eggs which have very thick shells and are tough to open. These enterprising birds have also been seen using twigs as tools to gather wool for their nests.

Tanimbar Corella

Tanimbar Corellas (also known as Goffin's Cockatoos) are capable of inventing their own tools and have even been shown by scientists to make different tools with separate functions to use in a sequence to collect the seeds they want to eat. Some birds have proved themselves sophisticated enough to plan ahead, by carrying their beak-made toolset with them to use later.

New Caledonian Crow

In the wild, New Caledonian Crows are one of the cleverest tool-making birds. They have benefitted from living on an island with very few predators, which has given them plenty of time to learn some astounding skills. When they are young, their parents teach them how to construct three different tool 'designs' to extract fat, juicy grubs from holes in trees. These tools are made using leaves from a specific plant called the pandanus tree. It takes almost two years to really perfect their tool making, but they become so skilful that they can copy the design of a tool without using the exact same technique to make it. Each of the three tool types have different uses, but the hooked ones have the highest value to the crows, being ten times more effective at catching grubs. The crows carry the best tools around with them and will wedge them safely into a crack in a branch while they eat.

In captivity, these clever birds can assemble tools from separate parts without being shown how to do so. This involves the ability to picture the finished tool in their minds and is something humans only learn to do when they are a few years old. It is a feat once thought only possible in the animal kingdom by apes, but these feathered brainboxes have proved that wrong.

Named after the secret agent James Bond, 007 is a wild New Caledonian Crow who proved to be a genius problem-solver. In a complex experiment, 007 had to solve an eight-step puzzle which could only be completed if all the steps were performed in the correct order and in under three minutes. The brilliant 007 worked out what needed to be done, including the use of different tools, and earned his food reward in record time. Having proved just how clever a bird can be, 007 was later released back into the wild.

Carrion Crow

In Japan, there are some Carrion Crows who have learned how to use cars to crack nuts for them. They wait for the traffic lights to change to red when all the cars stop. Then they place a nut in the perfect spot on the crossing. Next they fly back up to watch as the lights change again and the cars roll over the nut, releasing a nutritious reward.

Sharing information is key to a crow's survival in the wild. Crows can remember a specific person's face. If a person is particularly threatening, they will pass the information to other members of the flock and even down the generations. Up to five years later, the descendants of the original crow will react with shrieking and swooping at the same 'threatening' person even though they have never seen them before. This can only be because they learned about them from the older generation.

Crows are bold birds and have been known to form relationships with people. They will leave 'thank you presents' such as shiny pieces of litter, beads or bottle tops for people who leave peanuts out for them.

Intelligent Investigators

Investigation, nosiness and clever curiosity about the world around them is what makes these birds so smart. They all want to dig deeper and aren't shy about looking for answers, often showing great patience and determination. Here are some great examples, which show that being curious, asking questions and trying things out is a brilliant way to learn and always a sign of real intelligence.

Eurasian Jackdaw
Europe, Western Asia, North Africa

Black-billed Magpie
Europe, Asia

Striated Caracara
Falkland Islands, South America

Herring Gull
Europe

Kea
New Zealand

African Grey Parrot
West and Central Africa

Eurasian Jackdaw

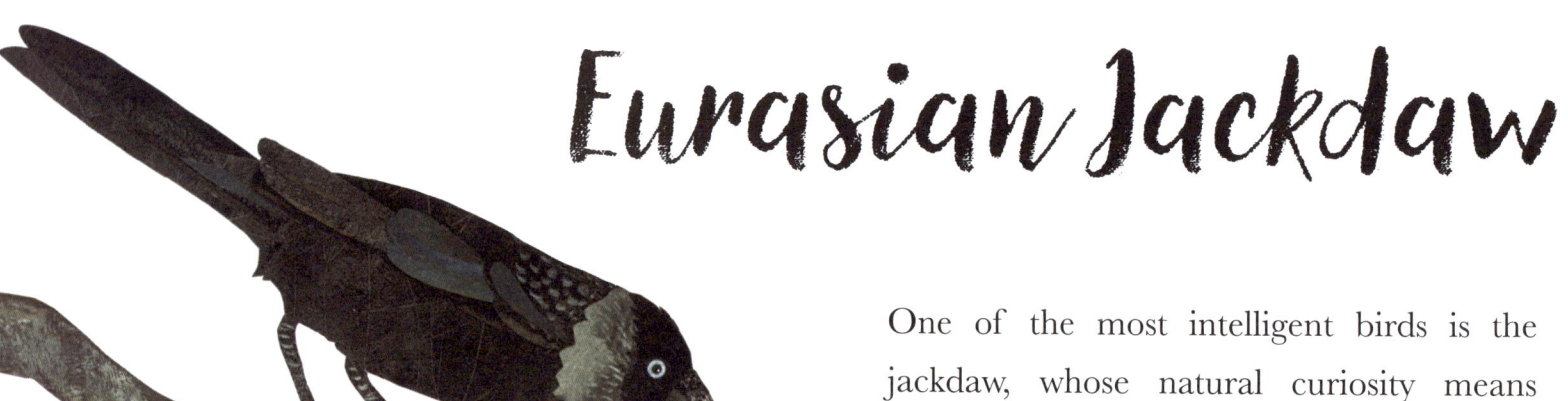

One of the most intelligent birds is the jackdaw, whose natural curiosity means they are quick to learn. They often make bonds with humans; one tame jackdaw was even taught how to steal money from a cash machine. Jackdaws can remember individuals and love to make eye contact with their distinctive pale grey eyes.

Black-billed Magpie

Another clever corvid, magpies can recognise their own reflection. In an experiment, they had a red sticker placed on their chest, which they attempted to remove from their own chest rather than peck at the mirror, proving that they knew the sticker was on themselves rather than on the bird in the mirror. This is something that very few animals are capable of understanding. Even human babies cannot recognise themselves until they are eighteen months old.

Striated Caracara

These characterful birds live in flocks and might be considered among the cleverest birds of prey. Their natural curiosity can find them searching for food by turning over rocks on the beach – or by rifling through the pockets and backpacks of tourists. They have no fear of humans, and one Caracara even learned how to use a form of vending machine to collect a treat of food.

Herring Gull

Gulls are inquisitive, bold birds with relatively large brains which help them respond quickly to changes in their environment. They live for a long time, which means they can build up memories of where and how to find food and share this knowledge with their offspring. Gulls can also read human body language and will only steal food if they think no-one is watching them. That is how they manage to snatch a chip from an unsuspecting tourist.

Gulls generally visit lots of different locations for their food and go to the same places at the same times, when they know food will be available. For example, they will wait for playtime in a school playground to see if the children drop any scraps of food.

One particular gull, nicknamed Steven, worked out that the local supermarket was an excellent place to find a meal. He learned to time his entrance and exit perfectly with the automatic doors to regularly help himself to packets of crisps kept near the entrance.

Another clever gull realised it could hitch a lift on the back of a rubbish truck a couple of times rather than having to fly the 120 kilometres to and from the landfill site for a meal, as it had been doing: much more convenient, and a great way of saving precious energy.

Herring Gulls have been observed 'fishing' for goldfish in a pond using pieces of bread as bait, and they can judge just the right height from which to drop clams and mussels so that the shells crack open perfectly.

And if you see a gull stamping on the ground, they are imitating the sound of falling rain, which entices earthworms up for water and gives the gull a juicy snack. These clever birds demonstrate real brainpower in the different ways they work out how to find food.

Kea

Keas are clever, inquisitive and full of personality. They love to play rough-and-tumble games with each other. On the ground they walk with a rolling waddle, but in the air they are acrobatic and poised, swooping, twisting and even hovering in mid-air, seemingly just for the joy of it.

The name Kea comes from their call, 'Key-Ah! Key-Ah!' and they also have a chuckling call which is just as infectious as human laughter: when one Kea 'chuckles', it is a signal for everyone to start playing.

Their playful intelligence is demonstrated by a very long childhood: up to the age of four, young Kea are indulged by the elders of their group and can get away with anything, including teasing and pinching food from the other birds.

Keas are fascinated by people and like to stick their big agile beaks and claws into everything they find, which can make them a real nuisance. They rip aerials, windscreen wipers and rubber trim off cars, open tourists' backpacks and even steal money.

One bird called Bruce was rescued as a youngster because he was missing most of the top half of his beak. He soon cleverly adapted, by finding a novel way to preen himself using a stone to rub against his feathers as other birds do with their beaks.

In another example of tool use, wild Kea whittle sticks and use them to spring traps set by humans to control pests. They've learned how to turn on water taps at a campsite and even managed to lock one unhappy camper in the lavatory. No wonder these clever, loveable clowns have the nickname 'naughty mountain parrot'.

African Grey Parrot

African Grey Parrots are thought to be as curious and clever as a human toddler, and Alex was one especially intelligent bird. He was bought by animal behaviour specialist Dr Irene Pepperberg so she could see just how much birds could learn. Irene started by teaching Alex the words for certain objects and gave him lots of praise and rewards when he was correct.

Alex quickly learned to identify different shapes, colours, foods and materials; he could even count to eight. Irene proved that Alex could use the words she had taught him and that he could also combine the knowledge he had gained. One day, someone brought a birthday cake into the lab. Alex didn't know the word for cake, but he did know the word bread, so when he tried a piece of birthday cake, he said, 'Yummy bread!'

Alex was really interested in anything new that came into the lab. He would ask, 'What colour? What shape? What is it?' He would even request a particular object or food if it wasn't visible by asking, 'Want corn! Want water!' If he was given something different, Alex would turn his head away and say, 'No'. Alex was actually communicating, not just 'parroting'; if he asked for a banana and was given a grape, he would throw the grape away and repeat, 'Want banana!'

No wonder Dr Pepperberg developed a close bond with Alex.

Terrific Teamwork

Sometimes working together is the best way to get results, whether to save energy, share and learn new skills, or to gather food most efficiently. All of these birds are smart enough to realise that they are better off working as a team rather than alone.

Raven
Northern Hemisphere

Harris Hawk
USA, Central and South America

Acorn Woodpecker
USA, Central America

Lance-tailed Manakin
Central and South America

Great Egret
Worldwide (except Australasia)

Northern Bald Ibis
Morocco, Syria, Turkey

Raven

Ravens often travel in pairs and will signal to communicate by holding up objects to show to each other and using their beaks to point in the direction they want the other bird to look. By working together they have a better chance of thriving in the wild and will even follow the other's gaze to see where they are looking. This ability to visualise what another bird is looking at takes great brainpower indeed and, ultimately, cooperating can mean greater success in finding food.

A Raven's brain is only the size of a walnut, but this is a large brain in comparison to its body size and ravens are said to be as clever as a seven-year-old child. These brainiest of birds have a wealth of talents, including planning for the future, tool use and mimicry, as well as exceptional problem-solving skills.

In some cultures, Ravens are known as wolf birds because they stay close to packs of wolves and have been known to work as a team. The ravens fly ahead to locate a carcass which may be too big to pick apart, then make a lot of noise to signal to the pack. The wolves follow and break the large animal down with their strong jaws so everyone can eat. Ravens even appear to form bonds with wolves; they play with the pups, will imitate howling and tease young wolves by nipping their tails, play tug of war and carry sticks around in their beaks for a game of fetch.

Ravens have excellent eyesight and a large part of their brain is used for visual information. In fact, their keen skills of observation are the secret to their success. They watch predators such as Arctic foxes hiding food. Then the birds wait until it is safe, before raiding the hiding spots and taking the foxes' food.

Most birds, including Ravens, will naturally fly away from loud bangs, but Ravens are so smart that they are drawn towards the sound of gunfire because they have learned that if there are hunters around there may be food left for them. They don't miss any opportunity to find food, and anything they can't eat, they will cache for later.

Harris Hawk

Most hawks are thought of as lone hunters, but these fearsome raptors have worked out that when food is scarce, it is better to work together. They hunt in packs from the same family, with the eldest female in charge. Each bird has a different role: either to block their prey's escape route, to flush them out of hiding, to chase them down, or to make the final attack. The rewards are then shared with everyone.

Acorn Woodpecker

Acorn Woodpeckers live in large family groups that all work together to store thousands of acorns in holes they have drilled into tree bark. The storage trees are known as granaries and can contain around 50,000 acorns. Everyone in the team has a job to do. The acorns must be gathered and then, as they shrink with age, be moved to smaller holes so they do not fall out. Other jobs include watching for thieving squirrels, warming eggs, feeding chicks or fiercely defending their carefully maintained stores.

Lance-tailed Manakin

Male Lance-tailed Manakins spend years perfecting their song and dance moves. These little birds work as a team, with the lead dancer performing for a female bird, while his chorus friends provide support and learn his moves. They spend all day practising so they can put on the best display, which includes acrobatic leaping and landing on branches, as well as singing and non-vocal whirring, clicking and popping, which comes from their wings vibrating together. It takes a lot to impress a female Lance-tailed Manakin.

Great Egret

Great Egrets and dolphins can be found all over the world, but it is only in the tidal salt marshes of South Carolina, USA, that a special kind of behaviour has been observed. The dolphins herd a shoal of fish through the water, forcing the fish to beach themselves, to make an easier feed for the dolphins. The clever egrets have learned they no longer need to fish for themselves, but simply wait for their food to be delivered by the dolphins directly onto the muddy bank.

Northern Bald Ibis

The Northern Bald Ibis has been extinct in the wild in Europe for more than 300 years. But in an example of teamwork between humans and birds, small numbers have been bred in wildlife parks and gradually reintroduced to the wild.

When the first flock of these reintroduced birds tried to migrate, they didn't know the route over the mountains south for winter, and sadly didn't survive the trip. So the next group were encouraged to imprint onto someone who became like their parent and taught them when and

where to fly. The first person whom the chicks saw when they hatched became this 'parent', who then fed them and let them follow them everywhere. When it was time, the pretend parent flew a microlight aircraft, which the birds dutifully followed.

When birds fly in a V formation, the whole group saves both time and energy, so they can all travel further than a bird flying alone. The arrow shape cuts through the invisible wall of air and the birds travelling behind get an easier flight. Being at the front takes the most energy, so each bird takes its turn to lead before moving to the back for a rest.

It takes really precise flying to maintain the correct distance from the bird in front. Each bird beats its wings in the opposite pattern to the one they are following, so as one bird flaps up, the one behind flaps down. They must all synchronise with each other for the V to work, and in the wild such skill is learned by observing more experienced birds.

At first, the technique of the hand-reared birds was terrible and they flapped all over the place. But with lots of practice, they gradually learned to fly as a team.

Eventually, the reintroduced flock of Ibis followed the microlight all the way across the Alps to the warmth of Italy. Thanks to the patience of the pretend parents, more than a hundred birds have successfully established breeding grounds and they in turn have taught their offspring how to fly the same migratory route. A lovely example of bird brains and human brains working together.

Index

Acorn Woodpecker 85

African Grey Parrot 78-79

aggressive behaviour 23, 34

alarm calls 28, 33, 36, 40

anting 59

Arctic Tern 21

Australian Magpie 23

Barn Swallow 20

Black Heron 62

Black Kite 60

Black Palm Cockatoo 29

Black-billed Magpie 72

Blue Jay 59

Blue Tit 32

bowerbirds 46, 48-51

brains 12, 14-15, 82
   cerebral cortex 12
   hippocampus 16
   human brain 12, 14
   neurons 14, 19, 24

Brown Falcon 60

Burrowing Owl 61

Carrion Crow 68-69

Clark's Nutcracker 24

colour vision 22

Common Cuckoo 38-39

Common Hill Mynah 42

Common Starling 43

Common Tailorbird 53

communication 15, 26-35, 69, 78, 82

corvids 15, 56

  see also crows, Eurasian jackdaw,

  jays, ravens

Crested Lark 43

crows 14, 56, 66-69

cuckoos 34, 38-39

curiosity 70-79

dance display 86

delayed gratification 25, 63

drumming 26, 29

Egyptian Vulture 64

engineering skills 46-55

Eurasian Jackdaw 72

Eurasian Jay 25

Eurasian Nuthatch 58

evolution of birds 12

eyesight 19, 83

food

  finding 31-32, 58, 60-67, 69,

  74-75, 82, 83, 84, 87

  stealing 28, 36, 40, 74, 83

  storage 16, 24-25, 28, 85

Fork-tailed Drongo 40

Great Egret 87

Great Spotted Woodpecker 29

Greater Honeyguide 30-31

Green Heron 63

Green-rumped Parrotlet 32

Harris Hawk 84

herons 62-63

Herring Gull 74-75

Homing Pigeon 18-19

honey hunters 31

Horsfield's Bronze Cuckoo 34-35

humans, bonds with 31, 69, 72, 78

jays 25, 28, 56, 59

Kea 76-77

Lance-tailed Manakin 86

learning 12, 14, 21, 32, 34-35, 41, 44, 52, 62, 66, 69, 74, 78, 83, 89

Macaw 44-45

MacGregor's Bowerbird 48

magnetic field, Earth's 19

mate, attracting a 29, 36, 41-42, 48, 86

memory 12, 16-25, 74

migration 16, 20, 21-22, 88-89

mimicry 36-45, 48, 61, 75

mirror reflection, recognising 72

mobbing 35, 39, 83

navigation 15, 16, 18-19, 20-21

nests and dens 20, 23, 34, 35, 39, 46-55

New Caledonian Crow 66-67

Northern Bald Ibis 88-89

Northern Mockingbird 42

parrots 14-15, 29, 32, 44-45, 76-79

playfulness 15, 77, 83

Pygmy Falcon 55

Raven 14, 56, 82-83

Reed Warbler 39

Rhode Island Red Chicken 33

Rosy-faced Lovebird 55

Rufous Hummingbird 22

Satin Bowerbird 50-51

Sociable Weaver 54-55

Striated Caracara 73

Superb Fairy-wren 34-35

Superb Lyrebird 41

Tanimbar Corella 65

teamwork 15, 80-89

tool use 15, 29, 56-69, 77, 82

Vitelline Masked Weaver 52

Vogelkop Bowerbird 49

weaverbirds 52, 54-55

Western Scrub Jay 28

Whistling Kite 60

Woodpecker Finch 58

woodpeckers 29, 85